PHOENIX
from legend to reality

PHOENIX
from legend to reality

Michel F. Sarda

Photography
by

Ken Akers
Alan Benoit
Jim Cowlin
Tom Gerczynski
Fred Griffin
Jerry Jacka
Jeff Kida
Richard Maack
Jim Marshall
Michael Reese Much
Stan C. Obcamp
Rick Raymond
Michel F. Sarda
Mike Scully
Bill Sperry

Ralph Tanner Associates, Inc.
Publisher
Phoenix – Prescott

Copyright © 1988, Sarda Resources, Inc.
4610 North 40th Street
Phoenix, Arizona 85018

Library of Congress Catalog
Number 88-051013

International Standard Book Number
ISBN 0-942078-15-2

Published by:
Ralph Tanner Associates, Inc. Book Publishers
1661 East Camelback Road, Suite 250
Phoenix, Arizona 85016

Printed in Japan by Dai Nippon Printing
First printing November 1988

TABLE OF CONTENTS

ACKNOWLEDGEMENTS

For their gracious authorization to reproduce excerpts of their publications:
Princeton University Press (Saint-John Perse: Collected Poems)
Holt, Rinehart & Winston, Inc. (Robert Frost)

For their generous donation of photographs:
The Mansion Club
The Mayo Clinic
Motorola

Book design   Michel F. Sarda
Contributing Editor Donnalee Ray
Marketing & Sales   Donna Ray Associates

Text translations   French   Sarda Resources, Inc.
                     German   Sarda Resources, Inc.
                     Japanese   Translation Services, Phoenix
                     Spanish   Translation Services, Phoenix
Typesetting   Type Studio, Phoenix

For Donnalee

For Bruno, who shared with me those discoveries
For Philippe, who also will, one day.

This book illustrates a legend that has become a reality. It offers a sensitive outlook on one of the most attractive new cities of this world.

But the mythical rebirth of the Phoenix bird is also the story of a **renaissance.**

As such, this book is dedicated as a message of hope to all those who have experienced pain and suffering.

It is also dedicated to all those anonymous and beautiful people of Phoenix and the Valley of the Sun, whose care and love have helped others survive a deserted life.

Especially to you, **Betty Ryan,** *who founded the Faith House, and whose daily fight for human dignity, during the past fifteen years, has brought to your smile the beauty of your heart.*

Michel F. Sarda

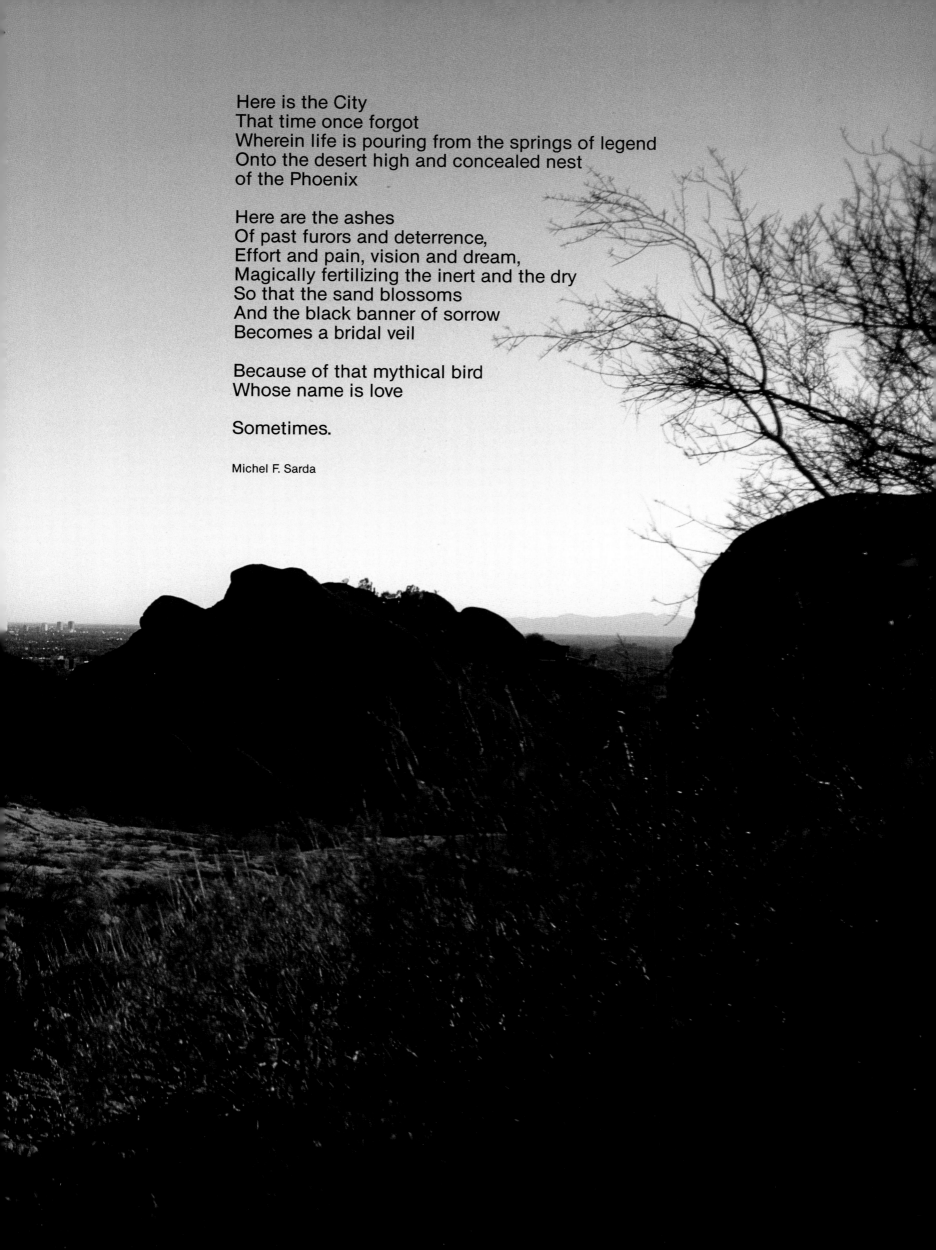

Here is the City
That time once forgot
Wherein life is pouring from the springs of legend
Onto the desert high and concealed nest
of the Phoenix

Here are the ashes
Of past furors and deterrence,
Effort and pain, vision and dream,
Magically fertilizing the inert and the dry
So that the sand blossoms
And the black banner of sorrow
Becomes a bridal veil

Because of that mythical bird
Whose name is love

Sometimes.

Michel F. Sarda

Paul Coze's Phoenix
(Alan Benoit)

About the Phoenix

The Phoenix is a mythical bird of unsurpassed splendor, which possesses the power, after consuming itself with its own heat, to come to life again out of its ashes. This strange bird appears in numerous cultures, from ancient Egypt (the Bennu Bird, or purple heron) to China (Tanniao- the Cinnabar Bird, emblem of the Empress). It belongs to universal mythology.

Phoenix is the Greek name this bird was given by the historian and traveler Herodotus, 500 years B.C.

The Phoenix is the symbol of the cycles of life, resurrection and immortality. It is the fire that both creates and destroys. It also symbolizes the sun's daily cycle, the red color, the summer season, the south.
(Dictionary of Symbols)

INTRODUCTION

At the threshold of a great new country
without title or device, at the green
threshold of a great bronze country...

Saint-John Perse

In 1984, I left Paris and a country where life is sweet and perspectives are mellow. I moved to Phoenix. This book is the result of three years of passionate interest for my city of adoption.

It wasn't long before it fascinated me. For whoever has traveled somewhat, Phoenix quickly becomes a magical and addictive place to live. Superb natural surroundings blend in a unique manner with business opportunities and a casual lifestyle. One's mind and energy are offered wide horizons. Here one can be or become either an artist or an entrepreneur, enjoy serenity or build an empire.

This range of possibilities best identifies a major city.

Most of the major cities of the world have been creatively explored by painters, writers, movie directors and photographers. Phoenix remained a surprising exception. One of the largest and fastest-growing cities in the United States, the capital of the State most visited for its natural wonders, the heart of the legendary West, Phoenix, more than many others, deserves such caring attention.

The active development of international relations also calls for a current portrait of this young metropolis, a portrait that would reveal its cultural identity, its fertile ethnic and social diversity, its spectacular economic growth – all qualities that designated Phoenix as one of the most promising communities of the future in John Naisbitt's *Megatrends.*

It is the purpose of this book to contribute to this portrait in an artistic and sensitive manner.

Phoenix, what a fabulous name for a town! And what a history already! Named barely more than a century ago by an English aristocrat, built over a revived network of canals whose origin is lost in a remote past, the city has sprung from the desert like a challenge. Here, at the beginning, there were no rivers boats could use, no sea harbor, no crossroad. Just opportunity and potential. Could Lord Darrell Duppa have chosen a better name?

A city constantly in the making. A metropolis, with the familiar pattern of avenues and buildings, the breathing of a powerful machine at work. And nature impressively present; not some of those narrow parks, without soul or mystery, dug out of the middle of some cities, like overgrown planters. Here we talk of entire mountain ranges, canyons, where body and mind freely escape.

And people. Because a city is first a gathering of people. People coming from the North, the East and the South, people from beyond the oceans, along with those who belong to this land. Different traditions and cultures fuel the dynamics of the community. From the melting pot a brighter sun rises.

Because the image to convey is sharp and luminous, the presentation of this book has been kept simple. People in their difference and specificity are illustrated by the timeless beauty of children. The presence of the desert, the theme of water, are more suggested than described.

Of course, native Phoenicians may not recognize in this book the city they grew up with. This vision is that of an artistic explorer, selective, unfair sometimes though respectful, always passionately subjective. An impression is not a survey.

Time is signing this book like the portrait of a living model. And like brushstrokes of a new portrait to come, major projects are underway which will shine in the future skyline, that could not be represented here: the Phoenix Municipal Government Center, Patriot Square, the Herberger Theater, Sky Harbor's Terminal 4, the Phoenician and Ritz-Carlton hotels. I cannot list them all.

Many people have contributed to this book, and they receive here my grateful acknowledgement; with special attention to the talented photographers who shared their time and enthusiasm with me. This includes the professionals whose photographs could not be selected for the purpose of this book. My thanks to Nancy Laswick (The Stock Option) and Jude Westlake (Visual Images West) for their friendly cooperation. And I cannot conclude this introduction without saluting the memory of my compatriot Paul Coze, whose talent and personality now belong to the legend of this town.

Michel F. Sarda

(Tom Gerczynski)

LEGEND

What is this city under a purple sky
Whose lights are nightly caravans
Trading the memory of the sun...

(Pages 18-19)
SUNSET POINT
(Michel F. Sarda)

Farther on, further up, where the thin men go on their saddles. . .
For a long time westward-faced
In a very high tumult of lands on the westward march.
In an endless unrolling of highlands at their highest flood. . .

Saint-John Perse

DESERT VIEW FROM PINNACLE PEAK
(Jim Cowlin)

This is a wild land, country of my choice. . .
Robert Graves

A MEMBER OF THE WISDOM DANCERS

This 16-member family dance group perpetuates the rituals of several Indian tribes. They performed for Pope John Paul II during his visit in Phoenix in 1987.
(Fred Griffin)

Like a great feat of arms on the march across the world,
like a census of people in exodus,
like a foundation of empires in praetorian tumult,
ah! like an animation of lips over the birth of great Books...
Saint-John Perse

(Opposite page)
PADRE KINO

A man of epic stature, Padre Kino founded several missions in Southern Arizona at the turn of the 17th century. The powerful statue which today faces the State Senate was offered in 1967 by the Mexican province of Sonora.
(Michel F. Sarda)

(Pages 24-25)
SUMMER REFLECTION IN THE ARIZONA CANAL
(Michel F. Sarda)

Men, creatures of dust and folk of divers devices,
people of business and of leisure,
men from the marches and those from beyond,
O men of little weight in the memory of these lands;
people of the valley and the uplands
and the highest slopes of the world...
Seers of signs and seeds, and confessors of the western winds,
followers of trails and of seasons,
breakers of camp in the little dawn wind,
seekers of watercourses over the wrinkled rind of the world,
O seekers, O finders of reasons to be up and be gone...

Saint-John Perse
Anabasis, translation T.S. Eliot

DUPPA'S HOMESTEAD

Darrell Duppa, a friend and partner of Jack Swilling in the restoration of the ancient Hohokam canal network, is credited with giving Phoenix its name. This English aristocrat, of international education and culture, lived in this adobe house (the oldest of its kind in Phoenix today) before being killed by Apache raiders.
(Michel F. Sarda)

Listen once more to the storm
labouring in the marble quarries of night.

Saint-John Perse

The sun buries his beautiful sesterce coins
in the sands, at the rising of shadows
wherein the thunder's pronouncement ripen.

Saint-John Perse

(Pages 28-29)
THUNDERSTORM ON CAMELBACK MOUNTAIN
(Fred Griffin)

Birth of a City
(Michel F. Sarda)

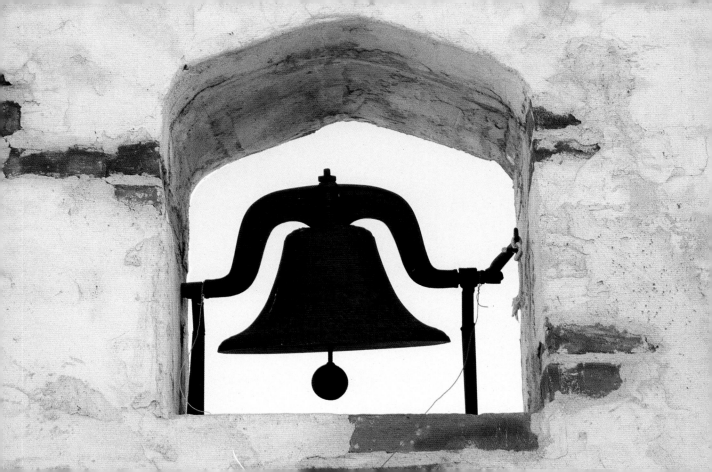

LEGACY

I hear the world reciting
The mistakes of ancient men
. . .

With their ever breaking newness
and their courage to be new.

Robert Frost

Built for Doctor Rosson by A.P. Petitt, a California architect who first introduced brick in a town made of adobe, the restored Rosson House illustrates the Victorian taste of the 1890s.

(Opposite page)
Built in 1979 to complement Heritage Square, Lath House won a national architectural award.
(Photos Michel F. Sarda)

A flight of pigeons competes with the Allegory which
adorns the copper dome of the State Capitol.
(Jim Marshall/Visual Images West)

(Opposite page)
In the solitude of Papago Park, Governor Hunt's Memorial
appears as a timeless landmark.
(Michel F. Sarda)

(Pages 38-39)
The Wrigley Mansion, former winter residence of the
Chicago chewing gum magnate, is now an elegant
private club.

(Tom Gerczynski)

(Left and above)
Originally built in 1929 to house the personal collection
of Maie and Dwight Heard, the Heard Museum offers
today one of the finest selections of traditional and
contemporary Indian art.
(Michel F. Sarda)

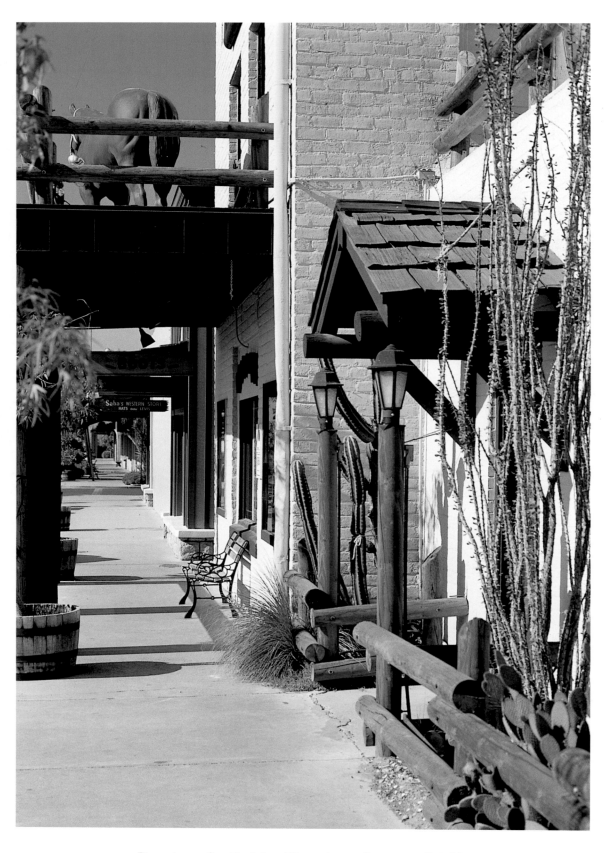

Downtown Scottsdale still captures the unpredictable
charm of the Old West.
(Michel F. Sarda)

Taliesin West was founded in 1938 by Frank Lloyd Wright
who discovered and enjoyed Arizona while contributing
to the design of the Arizona Biltmore Hotel. A foundation
now perpetuates the ideas and design concepts of the
master architect.

(Michel F. Sarda)

(Pages 44-45)
Grady Gammage Auditorium, on Arizona State University's campus in Tempe, is one of the last major designs
by Frank Lloyd Wright, inspired by original sketches for
an opera house in Baghdad, Iraq.

(Bill Sperry)

Tovrea Castle, (also affectionately termed the wedding cake) built in the late 20s was once occupied by cattle baron Ed Tovrea.

(Michel F. Sarda)

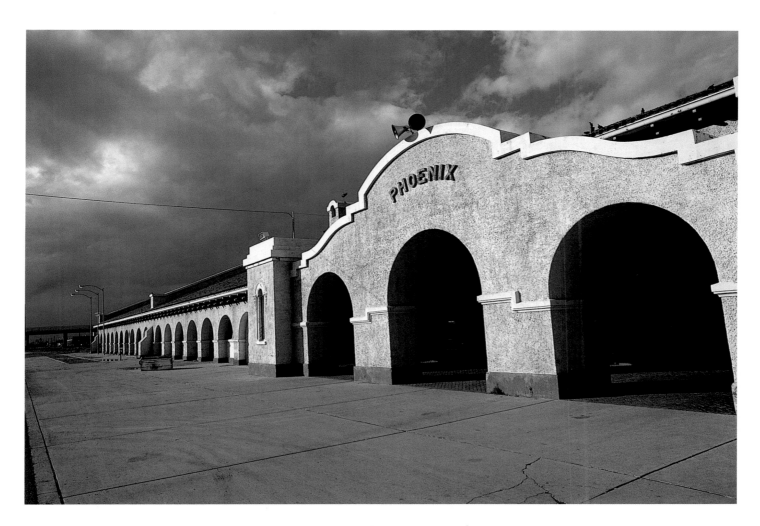

What exciting memories Phoenix Union Station could
revive...

(Bill Sperry)

(Pages 48-49)
AFTER THE SUMMER STORM
(Michel F. Sarda)

Out where the world is in the making
Where fewer hearts in despair are aching,
That's where the West begins;
Where there's more of singing and less of sighing,
Where there's more of giving and less of buying,
And a man makes friends without half trying –
That's where the West begins.

Arthur Chapman

A member of the Lydia Torea Dance Company which keeps the Hispanic tradition of flamenco dancing alive.

(Michel F. Sarda)

PEOPLE

Bring me men to match my mountains,
Bring me men to match my plains,
Men with empires in their purpose
And new eras in their brains. . .
Sam Walter Foss

(Pages 52-53)
Every year, the Valley of the Sun sets the stage for
major rodeos.
(Alan Benoit)

The smile of a child belongs to every culture.
(Bill Sperry)

A cowboy in the making everyone can relate to.
(Alan Benoit)

A purebred Arabian colt receives loving attention in one of Scottsdale's famous breeding farms. Every year, the Arabian auctions attract horse lovers from all over the world.

(Alan Benoit)

The Desert Botanical Garden reveals an unexpected and
exuberant flora.
(Michel F. Sarda)

(Pages 58-59)
Riders in the Phoenix Mountain Preserve.
(Bill Sperry)

The desert offers stunning surroundings to some of the
best golf courses in the country.
(Richard Maack/The Stock Option)

(Pages 60-61)
The combination of desert environment and imaginative
design has recently favored the creation of several
outstanding resorts, like the Boulders in Carefree.
(Jerry Jacka)

Windsurfers enjoy McCormick Ranch Lake in Scottsdale.
(Bill Sperry)

(Opposite page)
Gliding over Lake Pleasant, a favorite weekend destination.

(Fred Griffin)

At dawn, a balloon race is about to start from Fountain Hills, saluted by the world's highest fountain.
(Alan Benoit)

Elegant shopping at the Biltmore Fashion Park.
(Michel F. Sarda)

L'Orangerie, at the Arizona Biltmore Hotel.
(Bill Sperry)

Rehearsal at the Phoenix Symphony.
(Fred Griffin)

(Opposite page)
On Civic Plaza at night, John Waddell's sculptures reach
for the city lights.

(Alan Benoit)

Many artists have chosen the Valley of the Sun as their home. Scottsdale's numerous art galleries actively promote western and contemporary art. Here at work is the hand of Robert McCall, a Paradise Valley resident, famous for his NASA and science fiction works.
(Alan Benoit)

Cosanti is the poetic working and living environment the
visionary Italian-born architect Paolo Soleri has built for
himself in Scottsdale.
(Jerry Jacka)

(Pages 72-73)
The 70,000-seat Sun Devil Stadium, home of the Phoenix
Cardinals and Arizona State University's Sun Devils.
(Ken Akers)

74

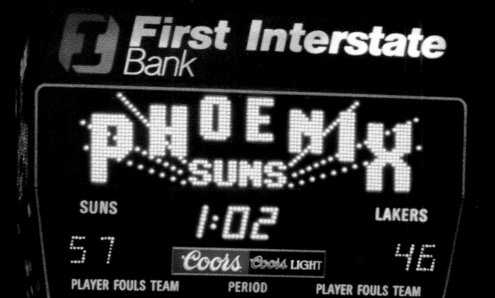

First Interstate Bank

PHOENIX SUNS

SUNS	1:02	LAKERS
57	*Coors* *Coors* LIGHT	46

PLAYER FOULS TEAM	PERIOD	PLAYER FOULS TEAM
5	2	4

TIME OUT

AVMC

Winston

FIESTA BOWL PARADE

With 40,000 students Arizona State University in Tempe,
ranks among the ten largest universities in the nation.
(From top left clockwise:
Jeff Kida, Michel F. Sarda, Jeff Kida, Jeff Kida
Opposite page: Alan Benoit)

ASU Campus.
(Michel F. Sarda/Jeff Kida/Alan Benoit)

(Pages 80-81)
The Arizona State Fair
(Bill Sperry)

Phoenix is one of the cities where Wright's work is best
represented. Here, the Lykes residence.
(Michel F. Sarda)

Outdoor swimming pools are natural and colorful
extensions of most Phoenician homes.
(Michel F. Sarda)

Children in Papago Park.
(Alan Benoit)

(Opposite page)
The banks of the canals send a natural invitation to
joggers.

(Fred Griffin)

Squaw Peak (above) and Camelback Mountain (right) are
not only superb and prominent landmarks in the core of
the city, they also are daily destinations for thousands
of hikers.

(Michel F. Sarda)

Dawn extends its rays over the expanding city.
(Bill Sperry)

The city is silent
Sound drains away
Buildings vanish in the light of dawn
Cold sunlight comes on the highest peak
The thick dust of night
Clings to the hills
The earth opens. . .

Tu Fu

GROWTH

Give thanks and clasp thy heritage –
To be alive in such an age!

Angela Morgan

Major corporations have their headquarters in Phoenix.
(Michel F. Sarda)

(Opposite page)
Downtown, where the heartbeat of the city is heard.
(Alan Benoit)

Sunset reflections.
(Michael Reese Much/The Stock Option)

All the dust the wind blew high
Appeared like gold in the sunset sky,
But I was one of the children told
Some of the dust was really gold.

Robert Frost

(Opposite page)
Central Avenue at dusk.
(Rick Raymond/Visual Images West)

Gracefully, St. Mary's Basilica contrasts against the Valley Bank Tower.

(Michel F. Sarda)

(Pages 96-97)
The Central Arizona Project brings the Colorado River waters to Phoenix and Southern Arizona through hundreds of miles of mountain ranges and desolate immensities.

(Jim Cowlin/Image Enterprises)

New silhouettes appear every day in the skyline.
(Michel F. Sarda)

In an ever expanding skyline, cranes are the drafting
instruments of the future.
(Bill Sperry)

FUTURE

(Pages 104-105)
Within a few years a spectacular network of new
freeways will irrigate the city.
(Richard Maack/The Stock Option)

103

Where light becomes architecture. . .
(Rick Raymond/Visual Images West)

New buildings will write the chronicles of a community,
like palm trees herald an oasis.
(Tom Gerczynski)

(Pages 108-109)
Communication with the outer world will intensify. . .
(Bill Sperry)

The third Mayo Clinic in the world will provide state-of-the-art medical diagnostic services.
(Stan Obcamp/Mayo Clinic)

Like Henry Moore's "Maternity" in front of the Biltmore Commerce Center, art will complement the business environment.

(Michel F. Sarda)

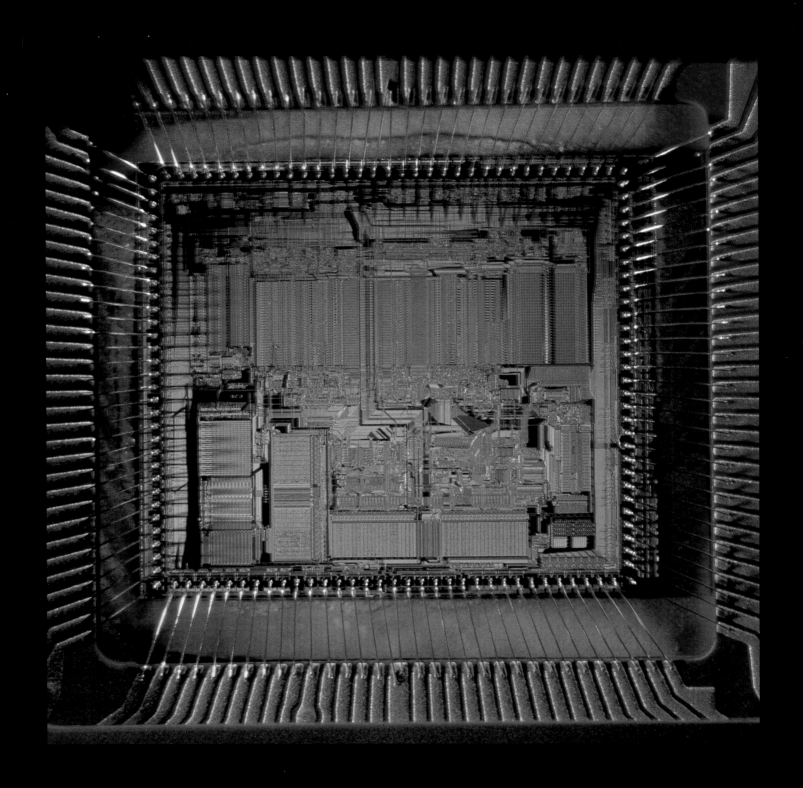

Both the new 68030 Motorola microprocessor, developed in Phoenix, and Downtown at night, create fantastic cityscapes in their respective scale.
(Above/Bill Sperry and left/Motorola)

Energy can generate beauty – like the coolers of Palo
Verde, the nuclear power station located 40 miles west
of Phoenix.

(Alan Benoit)

Audacious design will shape tomorrow's environment.
(Michel F. Sarda)

(Pages 116-117)
The Herberger Theater, under construction, provides a
backdrop for John Waddell's figures as they perform a
graceful and silent dance.
(Michel F. Sarda)

There are eyes so full of dreams
That they show us scenes of yore;
Eyes whose pensive glances pour
Light of other skies and dreams. . .

Antonio Gomes Restrepo

(Bill Sperry)

What is for me ahead
In life's merry-go-round?
It's a colorful and musical world
And my look will make beautiful
All that's for me ahead.

Michel F. Sarda

INDEX

Page 16

Phoenix à l'aube.

Phoenix al amanecer.

Sonnenaufgang über Phoenix.

フェニックスの夜明け

Pages 18-19

Sunset Point

Vista Panorámica
de la Puesta del Sol.

Aussichtspunkt Sonnenuntergang
Sunset Point.

日没の地点

Page 20

Desert vu depuis Pinnacle Peak.

Vista del desierto desde
Pinnacle Peak.

Blick auf die Wüste von
"Pinnacle Peak".

ピナクル山頂からの砂漠展望

Page 21

"Danseur de la Sagesse"
Cette famille de seize membres, con-
stituée en compagnie de danse,
perpétue les rituels de plusieurs tribus
indiennes.

Un miembro de Wisdom Dancers. Este
grupo familiar de baile de 16 miembros
perpetúa los rituales de muchas Tribus
Indias.

"Der Weissheits Tanzer"
Diese Tanzgruppe besteht aus einer 16
köpfigen Familie und verewigt die
ritualen Tänze mehrerer Indianer
Stamme.

賢いダンサー。この16名からなる民族ダン
スグループは数々のインディアン部族の伝
統を継承している。彼らは1987年にローマ
法皇パウロ2世がフェニックスを訪れた際
に、法皇のためにダンスを演じた。

Page 22

Personnage d'épopée, le père Kino a
établi plusieurs missions catholiques
au sud de l'Arizona, au début du 17ème
siecle.

Un hombre de talla epica, el Padre
Kino fundó varias misiones Católicas
en el Suroeste de Arizona, a finales del
Siglo XVII.

Vater Kino, ein mann heroischer
Statur, gründete mehrere katholische
Missionen in Süd Arizona, um die 17.
Jahrhundertswende.

17世紀が変わろうとした時に、南部アリゾ
ナで数々の布教の礎を築いたペドレ・キノ
の勇姿。ソノラのメキシカン地域から提供
されたこの勇壮な立像は、州の上院議会に
面している。

Pages 24-25

Reflets de l'été dans un des
canaux de Phoenix.

Reflexión de verano en el
canal de Arizona.

Sommerreflexionen im
Arizona Kanal.

アリゾナ運河の夏の反照

Page 27

La maison de Duppa. Darrell Duppa, ami et partenaire de Jack Swilling dans l'en-
treprise de restauration des canaux construits par la tribu Hohokam dans des
temps reculés, passe pour avoir donné son nom à la ville de Phoenix. Cet
aristocrate anglais, d'education et de culture internationales, a vecu dans cette
maison d' "adobe" (terre crue) — aujourd'hui la plus ancienne de ce type à
Phoenix - avant d'être tué par des maraudeurs apaches.

Duppa's Homestead. Darrel Duppa, un amigo y socio de Jack Swilling en la
restauracion de la antigua red del canal Hohokam, se le acredita por darle a
Phoenix su nombre. Este aristocrata ingles, de educacion y cultura internacional,
vivió en esta case de adobe (la mas antigua en su clase en Phoenix hoy dia) antes
de ser asesinado pcr los Apaches.

Heimstätte Duppas. Darrel Duppa, ein Freund und Partner von Jack Swilling, wird
die Anerkennung gegeben nicht nur Phoenix seinen Namen gegeben zu haben,
sondem auch die Restaurationsarbeiten an der uralten Hohokam Kanalnetzwerke
vollbracht zu haben. Dieser Englische Aristokrat, mit Internationaler Ausbildung
und Kultur, lebte in diesem Adobe Haus, das älteste dieser Art im heutigem
Phoenix, bis er von Apache indianern getötet wurde.

ダバの自作農場。古代のホホカム運河の復旧事業でジャック・スウィリングの友人で協力
者であったダレル・ダパは、フェニックスの名付け親としての名誉を与えられている。

Pages 28-29

Orage sur Camelback.

Tormenta en la Montaña Camelback.

Gewitter über Camelback Mountain.

カメルバック山の激しい雷雨

Page 31

Naissance d'une cité.

El nacimiento de una ciudad.

Geburt einer Stadt.

市の誕生。

Page 32

La cloche des âges.

Campana de los años.

Die Glocke des Zeitalters.

年代の鐘

Page 34

Construite pour le Docteur Rosson par A.P. Petitt, un architecte de Californie qui le premier introduisit la brique dans une ville faite d' "adobe", cette maison récemment restaurée illustre le goût de la fin du siecle dernier.

Construida para el Doctor Rosson por A.P. Petitt, un arquitecto californiano, quien fuera el primero en introducir el ladrillo en un pueble hecho de adobe, las casa restaurada Rosson muestra el gusto Victoriano de los años de 1890.

Gebaut für Doktor Rosson von A.P. Petitt, ein Architekt aus Kalifornien der zuerst Ziegel in eine Stadt brachte die vorwieglich mit luftgetrocknetem Ziegelstein (Adobe) baute.

最初にアドービ造りの町にレンガを導入した、カリフォルニアの建築家 A.P. ペティットによってロッソン博士のために建てられ、修復されたロッソンハウスには1890年代のビクトリア様式が示されている。

Page 35

Construit en 1979 pour compléter Heritage Square, Lath House ("la maison de treillis") a reçu un prix national d´architecture.

Construida en 1979 para complementar Heritage Square, Lath House ganó un premio nacional de arquitectura.

Das Gitter Haus, 1979 gebaut complimentiert das "Erbschaft Quadrat" (Heritage Square), und gewann einen nationale Architekten preis.

1979年にヘリテージ広場を補足するために建てられた木摺の家は、米国建築賞を授与された。

Page 36

Un vol de pigeons vient tenir compagnie à l'allégorie qui couronne le dôme de cuivre du Capitole de l'Etat d'Arizona.

un vuelo de palomas compite con la Alegoría que adorna la cúpola de cobre del Capitolio.

Tauben umschweben in fliegender Konkurrenz die zierende Allegorie des Kupfergewölbes uber dem Kongressgebaüde.

鳩の飛行の美しさは、州都の銅円屋根の美しさを引き立てているアレゴリーと競い合っている。

Page 37

Dans la solitude de Papago Park, le mausolée du gouverneur Hunt apparait comme un repère hors du temps.

En la soledad del Parque Papago, el Monumento a la Memoria del Gobernador Hunt aparece como un punto de referencia perdurable.

In der schweigenden Ewigkeit des Papago Parkes erscheint das zeitlose Mausoleum des ehemaligen Gouverneur's Hunt.

パパゴ公園の寂しい場所で、ハント知事の記念碑は時代を超越したランドマークのように見える。

Pages 38-39

La Wrigley Mansion, ancienne résidence d'hiver du roi du chewing-gum de Chicago, a été transformée en un élégant club privé.

La Mansión Wrigley, antiguamente la residencia de invierno del magnate del chicle de Chicago, es ahora un elegante club privado.

Die Wrigley Villa; ehemalige Winter Residenz der Kaugummimagnaten aus Chicago, ist heute ein exclusiver Privatklub.

シカゴのチューイングガム王の以前の冬季邸宅であったリングレイマンションは現在、優雅な個人用クラブとして使用されている。

| Pages 40-41 | | Page 42 | Page 43 |

Destiné lors de sa construction en 1929 à accueillir la collection personnelle de Maie et Dwight Heard, le Heard Museum presente aujourd'hui une des meilleures collections d'art indien traditionel et contemporain.

Originalmente construida en 1929 para guardar la colección personal de Maie y Dwight Heard, el Museo Heard ofrece hoy una de las colecciones mas finas del arte tradicional y contemporaneo indígena.

Das Heard Museum offeriert heute die originellsten Kollektionen traditioneller and zeitgenössiger Indianerkunst. Es wurde in 1929 für die personlichen Kollektionen Maie and Dwight Heards gebaut.

1929年に、当初はマイエとドワイト・ヒアードの個人所蔵品の建物として建てられたものであるが、現在ではヒアード美術館として伝統的そして当代インディアン美術の最高級の収集品の一つを提供している。

Le vieux Scottsdale conserve tout le charme et l'inattendu du Far-West de la légende.

El Centro de Scottsdale todavia captura el encanto impredicrible del Viejo Oeste.

Die Innenstadt von Scottsdale (Downtown) bewahrt immer noch den reizvollen Charme des Alten Westens.

スコッツデイルの市街地は、いまだに、古い西部の予知できない魅力を持っている。

Maison, école et cabinet d'architecte, Taliesin West a été fondé en 1938 par Frank Lloyd Wright, qui avait découvert et aimé l'Arizona lors de sa contribution à la construction de l'hotel Arizona Biltmore.

Una casa, una escuela, una oficina, Taliesin West fue fundada en 1938 por Frank Lloyd Wright quien disfrutó Arizona mientras contribuía en el diseño del Arizona Biltmore Hotel.

Ein Haus, eine Schule, ein Arkitenktenbüro; Taliesin West wurde in 1938 von Frank Lloyd Wright gegründet. Während dieser Zeit, steuerte er bei dem Entwurf des Arizona Biltmore Hotel bei.

アリゾナ・ビルトモア・ホテルのデザインに寄与している間にアリゾナでの生活を楽しんでいたフランク・ロイド・ライトによって1938年にタリエシン・ウエストの家、学校、事務所は建てられた。建築基盤には今日この卓越した建築家の哲学と概念が永続している。

| Pages 44-45 | Page 46 | Page 47 | Pages 48-49 |

La Salle Gammage, sur le campus de l'Université d'Etat d'Arizona, à Tempe, est l'un des derniers grands projets de F.L. Wright, inspire par des croquis originaux pour l'Opéra de Bagdad.

El Grady Gammage Auditorium, en el campus de Tempe de Arizona State University, es uno de los últimos diseños principales de F.L. Wright, inspirado por los croquis originales para un teatro de ópera en Bagdad, Iraq.

Grady Gammage Auditorium, auf dem Gelände der Arizona State Universität in Tempe. Es ist eine der letzten Entwürfe bei F.L. Wrights. Inspirationen kamen von originellen Skizzen des Opernhauses in Bagdad, Irak.

テンピのアリゾナ州立大学のキャンパスにあるグラデイ・ガマージ講堂は、イラクのバグダットのオペラハウスのための最初のスケッチによって霊感を受けた、F.L.ライトによる最後の主要なデザインの一つである。

Le Chateau Tovrea (appelé aussi la "pièce montee") a été construit dans les années 20, et a été un moment habite par Ed Tovrea, un roi de l'élevage.

Tovrea Castle, (tambien carinõsamente nombrada como el pastel de bodas) construida a finales de los años 20, una vez fue ocupada por el baron de ganado Ed Tovrea.

Tovrea Schloss (Tovrea Castle) auch liebevoll der "Hochzeitskuchen" genannt, wurde in den späten 20ern gebaut. Ehemalig wurde es von dem Cattle Baron (Rinderbaron) Ed Tovrea bewohnt.

イースト・ワシントン・ロードのトブレア・キャッスル (これはまたウエディングケーキと愛情のこもった名前が付けられている) は20年代末に建てられたもので、一時大牧場主トブレア男爵が使用していた。

La gare de Phoenix semble remplie de passionnants souvenirs...

Qué recuerdos tan excitantes podría revivir Phoenix Union Station...

Phoenix Union Station (Bahnhof), welche errengenden Erinnerungen er in uns erweckt...

素晴らしい記憶を蘇らせるであろうフェニックス・ユニオン駅。

Apres un orage d'été.

Después de la tormenta de verano.

Sommergewitter.

夏の嵐の後。

Page 50

Un membre de la troupe de Lydia Torea, qui conserve vivante la tradition de la danse andalouse.

Un miembro de la Lydia Torea Dance Company, la cual mantiene viva la tradición hispana del baile flamenco.

Ein Mitglied der Lydia Torea Tanzgruppe. Sie erhalten die hispanische Tradition des Flamenco Tanzes.

現存するラテンアメリカのフラミンゴダンスの伝統を保存している、リディア・トレア・ダンス・カンパニーのメンバー。

Pages 52-53

Chaque année, Phoenix et Scottsdale accueillent d'importants spectacles de rodeo.

Cada año, Phoenix y Scottsdale son los escenarios de grandes rodeos.

Phoenix und Scottsdale veranstalten jedes Jahn die grossten Rodeos.

毎年、フェニックスとスコッツデールでは主要なロデオの舞台が設けられる。

Page 54

Le sourire d'un enfant appartient à toutes les cultures.

La sonrisa de un niño pertenece a cada cultura.

Das lacheln eines Kindes spricht die Sprache jeder Kultur.

全ての文化に相応しい子供の笑顔。

Page 55

Un cowboy en herbe, auquel chacun peut s'identifier.

Haciéndose un cowboy, con quien todo el mundo se puede identificar.

Ein cowboy von morgen.

誰もが親しめる修業中のカーボーイ。

Page 56

Un poulain arabe du meilleur lignage reçoit des soins affectueux dans l'un des haras de Scottsdale. Chaque année, les ventes de chevaux attirent les amateurs du monde entier.

Un potro de raza árabe recibe atención amorosa en una de las famosas fincas de cruce de Scottsdale. Cada año, las ventas arabes atraen a amantes de caballos de todas partes del mundo.

Ein reinrassiges arabisches Folen erhält Leibevolle Pflege auf einem berühmten Scottsdale Gestüt. Die jährliche Arabische Auktion zieht Pferde Liebhaber aus aller Welt an.

スコッツデールの有名な畜産場の一つで、可愛がられているアラブ血統の雄の子馬。毎年、アラブ馬競売場は世界中からの馬愛好家を魅了する。

Page 57

Le Jardin Botanique du Desert révele la plus inattendue et exuberante des vegetations.

El Desert Botanical Garden revela una inesperada y bella flora.

Der "Botanische Wüstengarten" lässt uns die überraschende der einmaligen Pflanzenwelt entdecken.

砂漠植物園は予期出来ないそして美しい植物を見せてくれる。

Page 58

Cavaliers dans le parc de Sauvegarde de la Montagne, au centre de Phoenix.

Montadores de caballo en Phoenix Mountain Preserve.

Reiter in der Phoenix Mountain Preserve (Heimatsschutzanlage).

フェニックス・マウンテン保護区のライダー。

Page 59

Le desert offre les plus surprenants decors pour quelques uns des meilleurs golfs d Amérique.

El desierto ofrece hermosos alrededores para algunos de los mejores campos de golf en el pais.

Einige der schonsten Golfplätze der Vereinigten Staaten liegen inmitten der natürlichen Schönheit dieser Wüste.

砂漠は、国内で最高のいくつかのゴルフ場に美しい環境を提供する。

Pages 60-61

La combinaison du desert avec une imagination d'architecte a fait surgir recemment plusieurs extraordinaires hotels de séjour, comme celui des Roches, à Carefree.

La combinación del ambiente del desierto y de diseños imaginativos recientemente ha favorecido la creación de centros recreativos excepcionales, como el Boulders en Carefree.

Das Zusammenspiel von Wüste und origineller Arkitektur hat letzlich zur Entstehung von prominenten Kurhotels beigetragen: wie z.B. "Bolders" in Carefree.

周囲の砂漠の組み合わせと空想的デザインは、ケアフリーのボウルダーズのようないくつかの顕著な保養場の新設に、最近では有利に働いている。

Page 62

En planeur au-dessus du Lake Pleasant, une destination appreciée des Phoeniciens pendant les week-ends.

Deslizando sobre el Lake Pleasant, un lugar favorito los fines de semana para la gente de Phoenix.

Segelflung über Lake Pleasant, ein beliebtes Ausflugziel.

プレザント湖上空のグライダー滑空は、フェニックス人の週末のお気に入りの行き先である。

Page 63

Les planchistes animent le plan d'eau du Ranch McCormick à Scottsdale.

Los windsurfers disfrutan del McCormick Ranch Lake en Scottsdale.

Windsurfers erfreuen sich am McCormick See.

ウインドサーファー達が、スコッツデールのマコーミック・ランチ湖で楽しんでいる。

Pages 64-65

Au petit matin, une course de ballons s'apprête à s'envoler de Fountain Hills, saluée par le plus haut jet d'eau du monde.

Al amanecer, una carrera de globos esta a punto de comenzar desde Fountain Hills, contemplada por la fuente mas alta del mundo.

Bei Tagesanzruch, Aufstieg zum Ballonrennen in Fountain Hills, begrüst von der höchsten Wasserfontäne der Welt.

夜明け時、世界最高地の泉に迎えられて、ファウンテン・ヒルズからの気球レースがまさに始まろうとしている。

Page 66

Le Biltmore Fashion Park offre un choix de boutiques élégantes.

Elegante "Shopping" en el Biltmore Fashion Park.

Elegantes "Shopping" im Biltmore Fashion Park.

ビルティモア・ファッション・パークでの優雅なショッピング。

Page 67

Le restaurant l'Orangerie, dans l'hotel Arizona Biltmore.

El Hotel Arizona Biltmore: el restaurante L'Orangerie.

"L'Orangerie", Restaurant in dem Arizona Biltmore Hotel.

アリゾナ・ビルトモア・ホテルにおけるレオランゲリエ。

Page 68

Répétition de l'Orchestre Symphonique de Phoenix.

Ensayo en la Sinfónica de Phoenix.

Probe bei der Phoenix Symphonie.

フェニックス交響楽団の練習。

Page 69

Dans la nuit sur Civic Plaza, les sculptures de John Waddell semblent vouloir cueillir les lumières de la ville.

En la Plaza Cívica en la noche, las esculturas de John Waddell alcanzan las luces de la ciudad.

Sehnsuchtsvoll strecken die Skulpturen ihre Hande gegen die nächtlichen Stadtlichter des "Civic Plaza". Skulpturen bei John Waddell.

夜のシビックプラザ、ジョン・ワデリの彫刻が市の明かりに手を伸ばしている。

Page 70

Beaucoup d'artistes ont choisi d'habiter dans la Vallée du Soleil. Au travail ici, nous voyons la main de Robert McCall, un resident de Paradise Valley, célèbre pour ses dessins pour la NASA et ses peintures de science-fiction.

Muchos artistas han seleccoinado el Valle del Sol como su case. Aquí a la obra esta la mano de Robert McCall, un residente de Paradise Valley, famoso por us trabajos de NASA y los de sciencia ficción.

Veile Künstler haben sich im "Tal der Sonne" ansässig gemacht. Heir, bei der Arbeit, ist die Hand des Artisten Robert McCall, Einwohner der Stadt von Paradise Valley; bekannt durch seine Werke für NASA und Science Fiction Gemälde.

多くの芸術家達は彼らの住宅地として太陽の谷を選んでいる。スコッツディルの多数の美術画廊は積極的にウエスタン・アートの奨励をしている。ここではパラダイス・バレイに居住しており NASA と科学空想芸術作品で有名なロバート・マッコールが仕事をしている。

Page 71

Cosanti est le lieu poétique que l'architecte ilalien visionnaire Paolo Soleri a construit pour vivre et travailler à Scottsdale.

Cosanti es el ambiente de trabajo poètico y habitacional que Paolo Soleri, el visionario arquitecto italiano ha construido para el mismo en Scottsdale.

Cosanti ist die poetische Arbeits und Lebensumwelt, die der visionäre, in Italien geborene Architekt Paolo Soleri für sich in Scottsdale gebaut hat.

スコッツデイルにイタリア生まれの空想的な建築家、パオロ・ソレリが建てたコサンチは詩的な仕事と住居の環境である。

Pages 72-73

Le stade des Diables du Soleil, qui peut asseoir 70,000 spectateurs, constitue la base de l'équipe des Cardinals et de celle de l'Université d'Etat d'Arizona, les Sun Devils.

El Sun Devil Stadium, casa de los Phoenix Cardinals y de los Sun Devils de Arizona State University.

Das 70,000 sitzige "Sun Devil Stadium", Heimat der "Phoenix Cardinals" und der Arizona State Universitats Sun Devils.

七万人の観客席を有するサン・デビル・スタジアムはフェニックス・カーディナルスとアリゾナ州立大学のサン・デビルスの本拠地である。

Page 75

L'équipe de basketball, les Phoenix Suns, joue à domicile dans le Veterans Memorial Coliseum.

Basketball - los Phoenix Suns en casa en el Veterans Memorial Coliseum.

Basketball - Die "Phoenix Suns" zu Hause im "Veterans Memorial Coliseum".

バスケットボール——彼らの本拠地、退役軍人記念競技場でのフェニックスサンズ。

Page 76

Groupes colorés et chars descendent Central Avenue - Danseurs Hopis - Quiconque l'a embrassée... - Le maire de Phoenix, Terry Goddard, participe a l'animation du defilé.

Grupos y carros alegoricos coloridos bajan por la Central Avenue - Bailarines Hopi - Quien le beso la mejilla... - El Alcalde de Phoenix Terry Goddard disfruta del participar en el desfile.

Fiesta Bowl Parade: Farbenfrohe Gruppen und festzugs ziehen langsam die Central Avenue entlang. - Hopi Tänzer. - Wer küsste ihre Wange. - Bürgermeister Terry Goddard ist gerne bei diesen Veranstaltungen dabei.

フィエスタ・ボウル・パレード（左上部から右回り）：カラフルなグループと山車がセントラル・アベニューを移動——ホピ族のダンサー達——誰もが彼女の頬にキスをした……——フェニックス市長テリー・ゴッダードがパレードに参加して楽しんでいる。

Page 77

Le defilé de Fiesta Bowl est le plus important du Sud-Ouest Americain.

El Desfile Fiesta Bowl es el mas grande en el Sur-Oeste.

Die "Fiesta Bowl Parade" ist die grösste im Sud-Westen Amerikas.

フィエスタ・ボウル・パレードは南西部で最大の規模である。

Pages 78-79

Avec plus de 40,000 etudiants, l'Université d'Etat d'Arizona, située a Tempe, compte parmi les dix plus importantes des Etats-Unis.

Arizona State University, con mas de 40,000 estudiantes, figura dentro de las 10 universidades mas grandes de la nación.

Mit mehr als 40,000 Studenten rankt Arizona State Universität in Tempe als eines der grossten Universitaten der Vereinigten Staaten.

四万人以上の学生数を擁する、テンピのアリゾナ州立大学は米国内で十大大学の中に入っている。

Pages 80-81

La Foire de Phoenix.

La Fiesta Estatal de Arizona.

Messe des Staates Arizona.

アリゾナ州博覧会。

| Page 82 | Page 83 | Page 84 | Page 85 |

Phoenix est l'une des villes du monde où l'oeuvre de F.L. Wright est le mieux representée. Ici, la residence de la puissante famille Lykes.

Lykes Residence (F.L. Wright 1966). Phoenix es una de las ciudades donde el trabajo de Frank Lloyd Wright esta mejor representado.

Lykes Residenz: Phoenix ist eine der Stadte die F.L. Wrights Arbeit am Besten repräsentiert.

ライクス邸宅（F.L.ライト1966）。フェニックスは、フランク・ロイド・ライトの作品が最高に表現されている市の一つである。

Une piscine ajoute comme une autre pièce, pleine de couleurs, à la plupart des maisons de Phoenix.

Las albercas al aire libre son naturales y coloridas extensiones en la mayoría de las casas de Phoenix.

Schwimmbecken sind eine natürliche und belebende ergänzung der meisten Häuser in Phoenix.

屋外スイミングプールは、ほとんどのフェニックスの家庭の自然でカラフルな拡張部分である。

Enfants à Papago Park.

Niños en el Parque Papago.

Kinder im Papago Park.

パパゴ公園の子供達。

Les rives des canaux sont une invitation au jogging.

Las orillas de los canales envían una invitación a los que gustan de correr.

Ufer weitläufiger Kanäle laden zum Joggen ein.

運河の提防はジョギング者達にとって自然の招待席である。

| Pages 86-87 | Page 88 | Pages 90-91 |

Squaw Peak et Camelback Mountain ne sont pas seulement de superbes repères au beau milieu de la ville, mais aussi le lieu quotidien de rencontre de milliers de randonneurs.

Squaw Peak y la Montaña Camelback no son solamente tierras magníficas y prominentes en el corazón de la ciudad, sino que también son destinos diarios para miles de escaladores.

Squaw Peak und Camelback Mountain sind nicht nur herrliche und prominente Wahrzeichen im Kern der Stadt, sie sind auch täglich Zielpunkte tausender Wanderer.

スクアウピークとカメルバック山は、市の中心部のただ壮大で有名なランドマークであるばかりでなく、それらはまた多数のハイカーの毎日の行き先きである。

L'aurore étend sa lumière aux confins mouvants de la ville.

El amanecer extiende sus rayos sobre la ciudad en expansión.

Der Sonnenaufgang über der sich ständig ausbreitenden Wüstenmetropole.

夜明けの光線は、拡張している市を越えて伸びている。

La tour de la Valley National Bank.

La torre del Valley National Bank.

Valley National Bank Tower.

ヴァレイ・ナショナル・バンク・タワー

Page 92

Des sociétés de dimension internationale ont leur siège à Phoenix.

Principales corporaciones tienen su sede en Phoenix.

Viele Haupt quartiere nationaler Firmen befinden sich in Phoenix.

各一流企業はフェニックスにその本部を持っている。

Page 93

Downtown, là où bat le coeur de la ville.

El Centro - donde el palpitar de la ciudad es claramente escuchado.

Statmitte - wo man den Puls der Stadt spüren kann.

市の鼓動がはっきりと聞こえる市街地。

Page 94

Reflets au crépuscule.

Reflexiones en la Puesta del Sol.

Widerspiegelungen im Sonnenuntergang.

日没時の反照。

Page 95

Central Avenue a la tombée du jour.

La Avenida Central en el crepúsculo.

Abenddammerung über Central Avenue

夕暮れの中央街。

Pages 96-97

Le "Central Arizona Project" conduit les eaux du Colorado jusqu'à Phoenix et dans le Sud de l'Arizona, sur des centaines de kilomètres, au travers de montagnes et de deserts.

El Central Arizona Project trae las aguas del Rio Colorado a Phoenix y al sur de Arizona, a través de cientos de millas de sierras montañosas y immensidades desérticas.

Das "Central Arizona Project" bringt das Colorado Flusswasser nach Phoenix und dem südlichen Arizona. Durch Bergketten und Wustenlandschaften fliesst es hunderte von Meilen bevor es am Ziel analgt.

中央アリゾナプロジェクトは、数百マイルの山々と広大な砂漠を越えて、コロラド川の水をフェニックスと南アリゾナへ運んでくる。

Page 98

Le Basilique Ste-Marie se découpe avec grâce sur la tour de la Valley National Bank.

La Basilica de Santa Maria contrasta con la torre del Valley National Bank.

St. Mary's Basilica kontrastiert anmutig mit der "Valley National Bank".

市の文化遺産を優雅に象徴している聖マリアのバリシカ聖堂は、ヴァレイ・ナショナル・バンク・タワーと結ばれている。

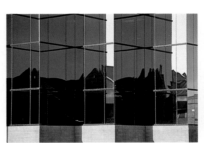

Page 99

L'horizon urbain s'anime chaque jour de silhouettes nouvelles.

Nuevas siluetas aparecen cada día.

Neue Silhouetten erschienen täglich am Horizont.

新しいシルエットは毎日空に描き出されている。

Pages 100-101

En quelques années, l'aéroport de Phoenix est devenu l'un des plus actifs du monde. Il est aussi reconnu comme l'un des plus sûrs.

En años recientes Sky Harbor se ha convertido en uno de los aeropuertos mas activos del mundo. También está clasificado como uno de los mas seguros.

Sky Harbor wurde in den letzten Jahren einer der verkehrsreichsten und zugleich sichersten Flughäfen der Welt.

近年、スカイハーバーは世界で最も活気があり、最も安全な空港の一つとなって来ている。

Page 102

Dans le ciel de la ville, les grues sont comme des instruments à dessiner le futur.

En la línea celeste de la ciudad, las grúas son los instrumentos de diseño del futuro.

Krähne am Horizont der Stadt zeichnen sich als Instrumente der Zukunft ab.

クレーンが未来のスケッチ用具となって、市の輪郭を空に描き出している。

Pages 104-105

Dans quelques années, un spectaculaire réseau d'autoroutes nouvelles irriguera toute l'agglomeration.

Dentro de pocos años, una red spectacular de nuevas autopistas irrigarán la ciudad.

Innerhalb einiger Jahre wird ein fantastisches Netzwerk von Autobahnen die Stadt durchziehen.

数年以内に新しいフリーウエイの壮大なネットワークが市を潤すであろう。

Page 106

Quand la lumière se fait architecture...

Donde la luz se convierte en arquitectura...

Wo Licht zur Architektur wird...

光りが建築物となる所……

Page 107

Sur de nouvelles constructions vont s'écrire les chroniques de la ville, tout comme les palmiers annoncent une oasis.

Nuevos edificios escribirán las crónicas de una comunidad, como las palmeras proclaman un oasis.

Nueu Gebäude werden die Chronik einer Stadt schreiben, so wie die Palmerbaume eine Oase verkünden.

ヤシの木がオアシスを案内するように、新しいビルディングはコミュニティの歴史に名をとどめるであろう。

Pages 108-109

Les communications avec le monde entier vont s'intensifier.

Las communicaciones con el mundo exterior se intensificarán.

Kommunikation mit der Aussenwelt wird sich intensivieren.

外部とのコミュニケーションは増大していく。

Page 110

La troisième Mayo Clinic au monde utilise les méthodes les plus modernes de diagnostic medical.

La tercera Mayo Clinic en el mundo proporcionará los servicios de diagnósticos medicos mas vigentes.

Die dritte Mayo Klinik der Welt wird uber die nuesten medizinisch diagnostischen errungenschaften verfugen.

世界で第三番目のマヨ・クリニックは、すでに開発された技術の医学診断サービスを提供することになる。

Page 111

Comme la Maternité de Henry Moore devant le Biltmore Commerce Center, l'art va pénétrer le monde des affaires.

Como la Maternidad de Henry Moore en frente del Centro Commercial Biltmore, el arte complementará el ambiente de los negocios.

Wie Henry Moore's Mutterschaft, von dem Biltmore Handels Zentrum, wird die Kunst das Geschaftsleben bereichern.

ビルテモア通商センターの前にあるヘンリー・モーアの母性のように、芸術はビジネスの環境を補完することになる。

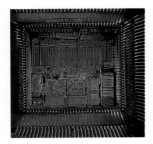   

Pages 112-113   Page 114   Page 115

Le microprocesseur 68030, dernier-né de Motorola (mis au point à Phoenix), et la vue nocturne de Downtown, chacun a son échelle, construisent de fantastiques paysages urbains.

Tanto el micro-procesador Motorola 68030 de vanguardia (desarrollado en Phoenix), como el Centro de la Ciudad al anochecer, en sus escalas específicas, crean fantásticas vistas.

Der erstklassige "micro-processor" 68030 von Motorola ist, der in Phoenix erfunden wurde, oder die Innenstadt bei Nacht, jedes in seiner Dimension erzeugt fantastische städische Gebilde.

2つの68030モトローラ最先端マイクロプロセッサーはフェニックスで開発された、そして夜の市街地では、それらの独特のスケールが空想的な都市風景を作りだしている。

L'énergie peut générer la beauté – comme les bassins de refroidissement de Palo Verde, la centrale nucleaire construite à 60 kilometres de Phoenix.

La energía puede generar belleza – como los enfraidores de Palo Verde, la estación de energía nuclear construida a 40 millas al oeste de Phoenix.

Energie kann auch Schönheit erzeugen – sowie die Kühler von Palo Verde, das Kernkraftwerk das 40 Meilen westlich von Phoenix gebaut wurde.

フェニックスの西40マイルの場所に建設された原子力発電所、パロ・ヴァーデの冷却塔のように、エネルギーは美を生み出すことができる。

Des formes audacieuses vont façonner l'environnement de demain.

Diseño audaz que le dará forma al medio ambiente del mañana.

Kühne Formen werden die Umwelt von morgen Zeichnen.

大坦なフォルムが明日の環境を形作っていく。

Pages 116-117   Page 119

Le nouveau theatre Herberger, actuellement en construction, constitue le decor devant lequel les personnages de John Waddell interpretent une danse toute de silence et de grâce.

El Teatro Herberger en construcción proporciona un marco para las figuras de John Waddell cuando ejecutan un baile gracioso y silencioso.

Das Herberger Theater noch unter bau, eine Hinterkulisse für John Waddell's Skulpturen im stillen und graziösen Tanz.

建設中のハーーバーガ　劇場は、彼らが優雅で静かなダンスを演ずるようにジョン・ワァデルの彫像のための背景を与えている。

Que trouverai-je demain dans le manege de la vie?
Un monde de couleur et de musique —
Et mon regard va rendre beau
Tout ce que demain me prepare.

Que hay para mi mas adelante
En el carrusel de la vida?
Es un mundo colorido y musical
Y mi mirada lo hara hermoso
Todo lo que hay para mi mas adelante.

Was steht mir noch bevor im Lebenskarrusel?
Eine bunte und musikalische Welt
Und mein Blick wird all das erschönen
Was mir noch vorbesteht.

私の未来には何がある
人生の回転木馬?
それはカラフルで音楽の世界
そして私の見るものは美を作り出す
それは全て私の未来にある。

130

CONTRIBUTING PHOTOGRAPHERS

Ken AKERS

A graduate of Arizona State University, Ken joined the Tempe Daily News in 1972. After working in Alaska for a time, he worked with the *Arizona Republic* newspaper from 1980 to 1986, during which he was twice elected News Photographer of the Year. Now working as a free-lance photographer, he has recently been designated as the Team Photographer of the Cardinals.

Alan BENOIT

Alan Benoit is a Tempe, Arizona based photographer whose work has been published in over 150 periodicals and books throughout the United States and in 7 countries. Benoit's work has also been used by many of the major corporations in Arizona and beyond. A member of the *Outdoor Writers Association of America,* Benoit was selected by Nikon for an exhibit entitled *The Great American Outdoors* at the Nikon House Gallery at Rockefeller Center in New York in 1988.

James COWLIN
(The Stock Option)

James has worked as a professional photographer since 1972. In addition to fine art photography, he owns a commercial photography studio – Image Enterprises – specializing in advertising and industrial photography. In 1977 he began traveling throughout Arizona and the Southwest to photograph the land. Most recently he has been exploring the unique qualities of the panoramic image. James is also a contributing photographer to *Arizona Highways.*

Tom GERCZYNSKI

Tom started his career in 1972 with Allen Dutton, a highly respected Arizona photographer. After deciding to devote more time to his teaching profession, Dutton handed his business to Tom. Since 1974 Gerczynski has been active as a commercial shooter, specializing in location and people photography. Each business has an asset and Tom considers Arizona one of his. Drawing clients in from every part of the country, he is able to offer an unlimited palette of locations to suit their every need.

Fred GRIFFIN

Fred's specialty, editorial photography, appears in publications internationally. He lives in Phoenix, Arizona, where he is a regular contributor to *Arizona Highways* magazine.

Jerry JACKA

While the work of Jerry Jacka appears in major publications around the world, he is best known for his contribution to *Arizona Highways* magazine – and he has gained a reputation as one of the leading photographers of the Southwest.

Jeff KIDA

Jeff started taking photos as a hobby while attending high school in South America, and continued at Arizona State University studying political science and photojournalism. He received an internship at *Arizona Highways* magazine in 1977 and has been doing assignment work for them since. For the past seven years he has been shooting advertising photos for the *Arizona Republic* while doing occasional news assignments. Since leaving ASU, Jeff has been a stringer for United Press International, Agence France-Presse, and continues to freelance for local and regional accounts as well as a number of airline magazines, including American, America West, Alaska, and PSA.

Richard MAACK
(The Stock Option)

Richard started his career in Chicago in 1975 as a fine art photographer, specializing in large format black and white photography. He has participated in group and one-man shows throughout the United States. In 1981 he moved to Phoenix, and in 1985 he started a commercial photography business, specializing in corporate location photography and architecture. Richard won two Prisma Awards in consecutive years, 1986 and 1987, from the Phoenix Society of Communicating Arts. He is a regular contributing photographer for *Arizona Highways*.

Jim MARSHALL
(Visual Images West)

Jim Marshall, a graduate of Brooks Institute of Photography with a degree in photo illustration, has been engaged in business nationally and in the Valley since 1980. His work is included in *Communication Arts Photography Annual, Graphis Photo 88,* the 66th Annual New York Art Director's Club and *Arizona Highways*.

Michael Reese MUCH
(The Stock Option)

Michael's photographic education includes military photographic training, as well as instruction in fine art photography at Phoenix college and Arizona State University. He started his career in the U.S. Army in aerial photographic reconnaissance. Service included one year in the Republic of Korea, where his duties included flying as a surveillance systems operator and as chief of the photo section. Upon his discharge, Michael came to Phoenix to work for a major aerial photography firm. In 1977 he opened his own photography business, specializing in architecture, editorial and product photography.

Stan OBCAMP

Stan is a commercial photographer, specializing in high-tech, scientific and consumer products in Phoenix since 1980. He has worked as a photographer for Mayo Clinic Scottsdale since 1987.

Rick RAYMOND
(Visual Images West)

Rick Raymond graduated in advertising photography from Northern Arizona University. A resident of Arizona for over 27 years, Raymond's work frequently appears in *Arizona Highways* and *Arizona Trend.* His corporate/editorial work recently won a silver and several merits in the 1988 Prisma Awards.

Michael SCULLY

Michael has been doing freelancing for United Press International, Agence France-Presse, *Arizona Highways* and the *Arizona Republic* before becoming a full-time staff photographer for the *Mesa Tribune* newspaper. He specializes in sports and spot news.

Bill SPERRY

Bill is a Phoenix-born freelance photographer specializing in editorial, corporate and travel photography. His work has been published worldwide.